Timeline of Pirates

Pirates have been plaguing the world's oceans for thousands of years. This timeline shows some of the most important events.

Gang-i-Sawai
Henry Every captures the *Gang-i-Sawai*, the richest prize taken by a pirate in the 17th century.

The "Jolly Roger" flag of the Flying Gang

Samuel Bellamy
Samuel Bellamy and 143 of his crew drown when their ship, the *Whydah*, is wrecked.

George Cusack
Irish pirate George Cusack executed in London.

Flying Gang
The first of the Flying Gang pirates make their base at Nassau in the Bahamas.

1577	1675	1690	1695	1698	1715	1717

Golden Age of Piracy
Adam Baldridge establishes a trading post on Isle St. Marie, Madagascar, marking the beginning of the Golden Age of Piracy.

Quedagh Merchant
William Kidd captures Indian merchant ship the *Quedagh Merchant*.

Blackbeard's ship
Blackbeard captures the slave ship *Concorde*, and renames her *Queen Anne's Revenge*.

Cruise around the world
Sir Francis Drake sets out on a piratical cruise and becomes the first Englishman to sail around the world. He completes his journey in 1580.

Continued at back of book

Things to find out:

DKfindout!
Pirates

Author and consultant: E.T. Fox

Senior editor Sam Priddy
Senior art editor Jim Green
Editorial assistant Kathleen Teece
Design assistant Rhea Gaughan
US editor Rebecca Warren
Jacket editor Francesca Young
Jacket designer Amy Keast
Managing editor Laura Gilbert
Managing art editor Diane Peyton Jones
Pre-production producer Nadine King
Producer Srijana Gurung
Art director Martin Wilson
Publisher Sarah Larter
Design director Phil Ormerod
Publishing director Sophie Mitchell
Educational consultant Jacqueline Harris

First American Edition, 2017
Published in the United States by DK Publishing
345 Hudson Street, New York, New York 10014

Copyright © 2017 Dorling Kindersley Limited
DK, a Division of Penguin Random House LLC
17 18 19 20 21 10 9 8 7 6 5 4 3 2 1
001–298649–Jan/2017

A catalog record for this book is available from the
Library of Congress.
ISBN 978-1-4654-5752-3

DK books are available at special discounts when purchased in
bulk for sales promotions, premiums, fund-raising, or educational
use. For details, contact: DK Publishing Special Markets,
345 Hudson Street, New York, New York 10014
SpecialSales@dk.com

Printed and bound in China

A WORLD OF IDEAS:
SEE ALL THERE IS TO KNOW

www.dk.com

Contents

Playing cards

Pirate ship

Pirate flag

Cleaning weapons

Telescope

Astrolabe

Gun

Barrels of rum

What is a pirate?

Everyone knows the legends of pirate treasure and wooden legs, but what exactly makes someone a pirate? Pirates tend to commit all sorts of crimes, but the one that matters is robbery. If you steal something out at sea, then you are a pirate! Pirates have come in many different forms, such as the three explained here.

Licensed to pirate

! WOW!

Pirates could still be **executed** under British law until **1998**!

Buccaneer

17th-century buccaneers mostly began as pig hunters who attacked the Spanish on the islands of the Caribbean. Soon they turned their attention to the high seas, using ships to move from place to place.

Illegal sea raider

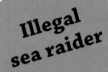

FACT FILE

» **Name:** Henry Morgan

» **Years active:** 1667–1672

» **Famous achievements:** With his skilled army of buccaneers, Morgan captured the city of Portobelo in Panama. He was later knighted by King Charles II of England!

Privateer

Privateers were a lot like pirates, but with one major difference. Instead of being criminals they were given permission by their country to steal from enemy ships during times of war!

FACT FILE

» **Name:** Robert Surcouf

» **Years active:** 1795–1808

» **Famous achievements:** Frenchman Surcouf successfully led a long and fierce battle to capture the *Kent*, a huge ship belonging to the British East India Company.

River pirate

Not all pirates operated at sea. Ships and boats on rivers were often poorly guarded, making them a tempting target for gangs of thieves. They would row out in the middle of the night to ransack the boats.

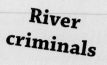

River criminals

FACT FILE

» **Name:** Sadie Farrell

» **Years active:** 1869–1870

» **Famous achievements:** Farrell led the Charlton Street Gang of the Hudson River, New York. They captured a small ship, called a sloop, and used it to raid boats and riverside areas.

Myth busters

The jolly pirates in many books and films are quite different to real pirates in the past, who were vicious criminals that robbed and killed people. Find out the truth behind piratical myths, from parrots to buried treasure.

Pirates said "Arr" a lot.

Pirates had hooks for hands.

All pirates owned parrots.

Pirates made people walk the plank into shark-infested water.

Pirates buried their treasure and made maps that would lead them back to the right spot.

Pirates sailed on great big ships called galleons.

Some pirates had huge ships, but most sailed on small vessels. Some even started out in rowing boats and canoes!

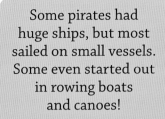

Buried treasure was incredibly rare. Treasure maps were probably invented in stories like Robert Louis Stevenson's *Treasure Island*.

Metal hooks were a replacement for lost hands in the past, so some real pirates may have had them.

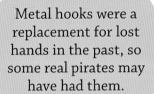

Planks were probably never used—pirates simply shot, stabbed, or hung people to get rid of them.

Actor Robert Newton seems to have invented the "Arr" sound for his roles as Blackbeard and Long John Silver in 1950s Disney films.

Some pirates kept cats and dogs onboard, while others may have kept parrots caught in the tropics.

Pirate hotspots

At one time or another, almost every stretch of water in the world has been home to pirates. Some seas were famously infested with vast numbers of pirates seeking rich treasure. Sailing through these waters as an honest merchant was a potentially deadly business.

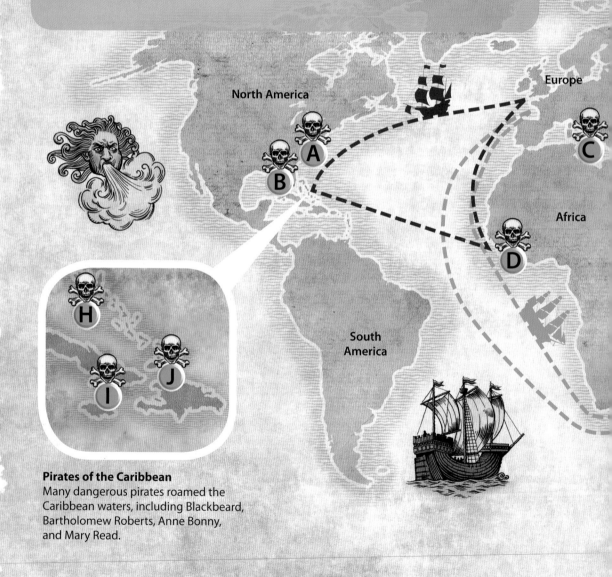

North America

Europe

Africa

South America

Pirates of the Caribbean
Many dangerous pirates roamed the Caribbean waters, including Blackbeard, Bartholomew Roberts, Anne Bonny, and Mary Read.

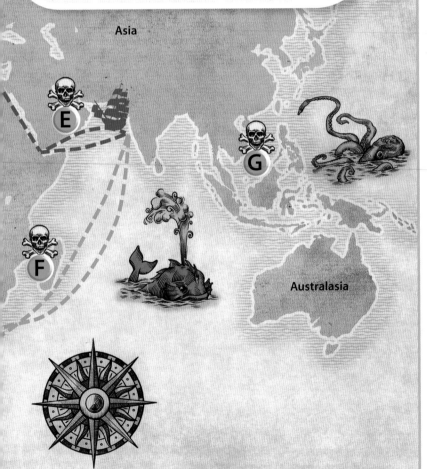

Trade routes
Merchant ships loaded with valuable cargo often traveled the same routes, making those areas popular with pirates.

- - - Atlantic: Ships carrying slaves, gold, sugar, and tobacco

- - - Indies: Ships carrying valuable spices and silks

- - - Hajj: Ships carrying wealthy pilgrims from India

Asia

Australasia

DANGER ZONES

A **American coast** Ships carrying cargo from American ports drew pirates here.

B **Caribbean** A rich trade in sugar, and plenty of islands to hide in, made the Caribbean a piracy hotspot.

C **Mediterranean** Barbary pirates from North Africa made the Mediterranean a dangerous place to trade for hundreds of years.

D **West African coast** Pirates sought slaves and gold being transported to and from West Africa.

E **Indian Ocean and the Gulf of Aden** Valuable cargoes of spices and silks put merchants at risk of attack.

F **Madagascar** From a base on Madagascar, pirates preyed on ships sailing in the region in the 1690s.

G **South China Sea** Pirates have infested this area for centuries, and still do!

H **Nassau** Between 1716 and 1718, pirates took over the Bahamas and made a base at Nassau's port.

I **Jamaica** Many 17th-century pirates stopped at Jamaica to repair their ships.

J **Tortuga** The lawless island of Tortuga was home to many pirates in the 17th century.

Sea Peoples

The Sea Peoples were a huge community of pirates that often attacked Ancient Egypt. Nobody knows where they came from, but they operated in the Mediterranean Sea between 1276 and 1178 BCE.

Battle of the Delta
The Sea Peoples tried to invade Egypt, as shown on this stone tablet, but were defeated by the Egyptian navy and arrows shot from the coast.

First pirates

When you think of pirates you probably think of 18th century buccaneers in the Caribbean, but the ancient world suffered from piracy, too. Ancient Egypt, Greece, and Rome all sent their navies to hunt down pirates. They were such a menace that some ancient myths even include tales of pirates.

! WOW!

Several **thousand** men sailed in the **Sea Peoples'** fleet.

GIU

Julius Caesar

Roman leader Julius Caesar was once captured by pirates, who requested a ransom before letting him go. Caesar thought the ransom was too low, and demanded they ask for more money!

Queen Teuta

The tribes of ancient Illyria were notorious pirates who attacked Roman ships. Queen Teuta ignored Roman officials sent to try and stop the piracy, but eventually surrendered when Rome sent an army.

Roman galley
Roman ships had oars as well as sails, and a pointed front for ramming into other ships.

Legends

A Greek legend tells of how the god Dionysus was captured by pirates. He turned himself into a lion and the pirates jumped overboard to escape. The pirates magically became dolphins in the water!

IO.CESARE

Barbary pirates

From the 16th to the 19th century, Muslim Barbary pirates terrified merchants in the Mediterranean Sea. Sailing from ports on the Barbary Coast (North Africa), they attacked trade ships traveling between East Asia and Europe, forcing captured sailors to row their ships.

! WOW!

Millions of European **slaves** were **captured** by Barbary pirates!

Sayyida was a powerful leader in Tétouan.

★ SAYYIDA AL HURRA ★

Pirate Queen of Tétouan

As a child, Sayyida al Hurra was forced to flee Granada, in Spain. She spent her adult life taking revenge on the country that had rejected her by sending pirate ships to attack European ships. She became Queen of Tétouan, in Morocco, in 1515 and was feared and respected by the Spanish.

Barbarossa was one of four pirate brothers.

★ BARBAROSSA ★

Barbary Pirate Admiral

Hayreddin Barbarossa was probably the most successful Barbary pirate. As well as terrorizing the Mediterranean in the 16th century, he was a trusted advisor to the sultan of the Ottoman Empire. He rose to become Grand-Admiral of the Ottoman Empire's navy and ruler of all North Africa.

Ward was also known as "Birdy."

JOHN WARD
⭐   ⭐

English Renegade Pirate

John Ward served in the English navy until he decided to join the Barbary pirates. He became a Muslim and led a successful pirate fleet from the city of Tunis, in Tunisia. By the time he died of the plague in 1622, Ward was a rich man who lived in a luxurious palace.

Danseker was originally a Dutch privateer.

SIMON DANSEKER
⭐   ⭐

Dutch Renegade Pirate

Danseker was another European who joined the Barbary pirates. He taught them the secrets of building European-style ships, which could sail far beyond the Mediterranean. His fleet captured more than 40 ships in two years. He was caught and executed in 1611.

Barbary strongholds

The major ports of Rabat, Algiers, Tunis, and Tripoli in North Africa provided safe havens in which Barbary pirates could sell their stolen goods.

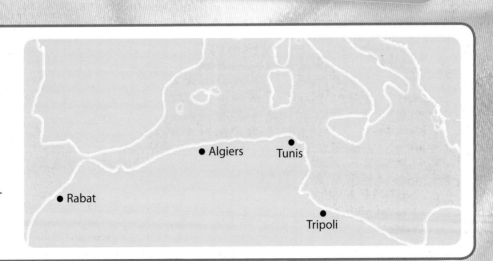

● Algiers   ● Tunis

● Rabat

● Tripoli

Privateer...

Few people have divided opinion quite like Englishman Sir Francis Drake. To some he was a hero—a privateer supported by the queen, who defended his nation and explored the world.

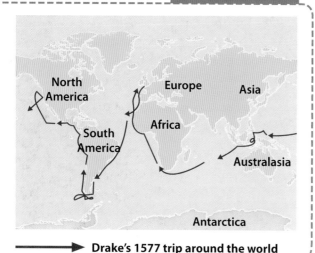

North America
Europe
Asia
Africa
South America
Australasia
Antarctica

Drake's 1577 trip around the world

Voyage of discovery

Drake led the first English voyage to circumnavigate (go around) the world. The voyage took nearly three years to complete.

Saffron

Turmeric

Cinnamon

Drake collected rare and valuable spices in Asia.

Queen Elizabeth I

Sneaky Elizabeth didn't publicly support Drake's piracy, but took a share of his treasure.

Golden Hind

After the voyage, Drake's flagship, the *Golden Hind*, became a tourist attraction in London. It was there for around 80 years before it rotted away.

A replica of the *Golden Hind*

...or pirate?

Many others, however, saw him in a different light. To them Drake was no more than a common pirate, a man famous for ransacking Spanish ships for all of their hard-won treasure.

TIMELINE

» **1540:** Born near Tavistock in England

» **1568:** Went on his first voyage to the Americas

» **1570–1573:** Led three voyages to Panama

» **1577–1580:** Led voyage around the world

» **1586:** Attacked St. Augustine, Florida

» **1587:** Led fleet to attack Spain

» **1588:** Helped defeat the Spanish Armada

» **1596:** Died near Portobelo in Panama

Nuestra Señora de la Concepción

Drake's greatest prize was a treasure ship, which he captured from the Spanish in 1579 by pretending to be a friendly merchant ship.

The *Concepción* carried 28 tons (26 tonnes) of silver and other riches.

Nuestra Señora de la Concepción

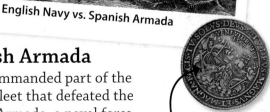

English Navy vs. Spanish Armada

REALLY?

Drake's nickname in Spain was **"El Draque,"** which means **"the dragon."**

Spanish Armada

Drake commanded part of the English fleet that defeated the Spanish Armada, a naval force sent to invade England in 1588.

A coin celebrating the Armada's defeat.

The Golden Age

The Golden Age of Piracy is the name often given to the years between 1690 and 1726, when pirates were found in almost every sea and on every major trade route. Many of history's most famous pirates were active during that time, including Blackbeard, William Kidd, and Henry Every.

WOW!

When piracy was at its peak, **more than 2,400** pirates sailed the world's oceans!

WHAT'S IN THE PICTURE?

1 **Small boat** Pirates left their ships on small boats to get onto victim ships.

2 **Cannons** Pirates used cannons to damage ships, but not sink them—a sunken ship wasn't worth anything!

3 **Pistols** Pirates often carried several pistols into battle. There might not be enough bullets in one, or time to reload.

4 **Easy capture** Damage from cannon fire to a merchant ship's sails made it hard for the ship to escape.

5 **Crew members** Pirate crews contained people from all over the world.

6 **Battle damage** Pirates would need to repair damage before the next attack.

7 **Fighting back** Pirates were kinder to victims who surrendered, but some merchant captains fought back.

Flags

For any sailor on a merchant ship, the sight of a black flag would have been terrifying, for it meant only one thing: pirates! A pirate flag was called a Jolly Roger, and pirates knew that if their's was scary enough, victims might surrender without a fight.

Skull and crossbones

This is the only genuine pirate flag left in existence. It came from a ship that sailed along the North African coast in the 18th century. It has faded over time, losing its black background.

Who's who?

Pirates sailing together in a fleet of ships might use the same flag, and many flew a skull and crossbones. However, sometimes they invented their own. This way, people knew from a distance which notorious pirate was sailing toward them.

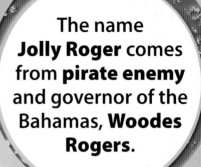

Thomas Anstis
Anstis displayed his nationality with a British flag, but added four grenades to frighten victims.

John Phillips
A dark fate awaited anyone who ignored the three symbols of death on Phillips's flag.

Thomas Nichols
If you saw this symbol today you would probably think it was sweet. To pirates, however, it represented death.

Bartholomew Roberts
Roberts's most famous flag showed him standing on skulls from Barbados and Martinique.

Samuel Bellamy
The sight of Bellamy's flag was often enough for a quick surrender. It showed a skeleton holding a trumpet and an hourglass.

William Moody
Like most pirate flags, Moody's used a variety of death symbols to threaten anyone foolish enough to resist him.

Jeremiah Cocklyn
The hourglass on Cocklyn's flag supposedly meant time was running out for his victims.

Howell Davis
The cannon and sword on Davis's flag warned that a violent fight faced any who didn't surrender.

Pirate treasure

Pirates hoped to capture glittering cargoes of gold and jewels, but they were more likely to end up stealing goods like sugar and spices. They could sell these items for money or swap them for other goods. Sneaky people didn't mind buying from pirates if it meant getting a good price!

Sugar
Sugar from the Caribbean had a very high value and could easily be sold to merchants for a good price.

Tobacco
Tobacco was one of the most common goods shipped from America to be sold in Europe, making it an attractive target for pirates.

Pieces of eight
Spanish coins could be used almost anywhere in the world. Many thousands of them were transported through the Caribbean.

! WOW!

An 18th-century cargo of **bird poo**, used to help plants grow, was once **captured by pirates!**

Slavery

Slaves were highly valued by pirates, not only because they were worth a lot of money, but also because they could be put to work on the pirate ship.

Christian missionaries negotiating the return of white slaves from Barbary pirates

Christian slaves
Barbary pirates raided European towns in search of white slaves to row their galleys or sell in North African slave markets.

African slaves in chains

From Africa
African slaves were worth a lot of money in the Americas, so they were sought after by Atlantic pirates.

Buried treasure

Pirates have long been associated with maps and buried treasure, but this is mostly because of Robert Louis Stevenson's 1883 novel, *Treasure Island*. In reality most pirates didn't bury their treasure, but that hasn't stopped hundreds of treasure hunters looking for it! In particular they focus their efforts on Captain Kidd...

Captain Kidd
Kidd did bury some of his plunder on Gardiner's Island, New York. However, it was dug up before he died.

Captain Kidd's map

Several treasure maps with strange drawings have been found that are said to have been made by the Scottish pirate William Kidd. Treasure hunters have tried to use them to find out the location of Kidd's plunder. However, they were probably forged (faked) by a collector of pirate artifacts called Hubert Palmer in the 1930s.

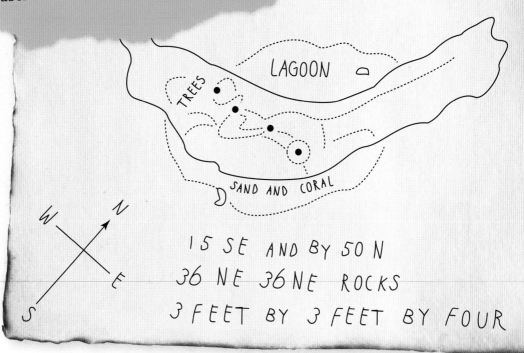

LAGOON

TREES

SAND AND CORAL

W N E S

15 SE AND BY 50 N
36 NE 36 NE ROCKS
3 FEET BY 3 FEET BY FOUR

Oak Island Money Pit

One theory is that Captain Kidd's treasure is buried in the "Money Pit," a mysterious hole in the ground on a Canadian island. Log platforms and stones with strange carved symbols are said to have been found by people digging down into the shaft. However, there is no evidence that these findings were real. The original pit may have simply been a natural hole.

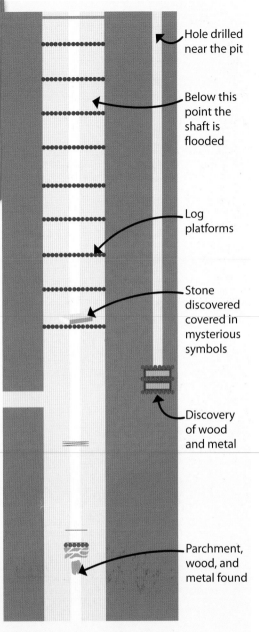

Hole drilled near the pit

Below this point the shaft is flooded

Log platforms

Stone discovered covered in mysterious symbols

Discovery of wood and metal

Parchment, wood, and metal found

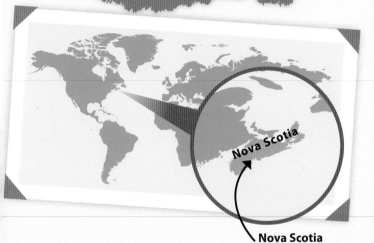

Nova Scotia

Nova Scotia
Oak Island is off the coast of Nova Scotia, Canada.

Roosevelt
Future US president Franklin D. Roosevelt visited the pit in 1909.

Treasure hunters

People have spent millions of dollars and their entire lives looking for buried treasure. Some have even died while exploring the Oak Island Money Pit, but no treasure has been found in modern times.

Pirate ship

Pirates used a variety of different ships. Small, single-mast sailing boats were popular for sailing around the Caribbean islands. But in the wide-open ocean, pirates usually preferred larger ships. They often changed their ship—if they captured a better one!

G

Flags aimed to intimidate other ships.

! **WOW!**

The largest pirate ship ever was the *Nuestra Señora de la Cabo*. It is thought to have had **100 cannons!**

Figureheads were purely for decoration.

PARTS OF THE SHIP

A   **Main deck**   Cannons were placed around the main deck. From this deck, several hatches led down to the lower decks.

B   **Quarter deck**   The ship's officers stood and gave orders from here.

C   **Hull**   A wooden frame covered in planks and sealed with tar formed the main structure of the ship.

D   **Rudder**   Ships were steered by changing the direction of a flat sheet of wood that was hinged to the back.

E   **Mast**   Pirate ships had up to three masts, each supporting a number of sails.

F   **Sail**   Heavy canvas sails caught the wind, driving the ship along.

G   **Rigging**   A complex system of ropes was used to control the direction of the sails.

Meet the crew

Pirate ships needed a lot of skilled men to carry out the various tasks onboard, and they needed to be well-organized. Sometimes pirates had a vote to decide who would fill the different roles, but usually they simply chose the person with the best skills and experience for the job.

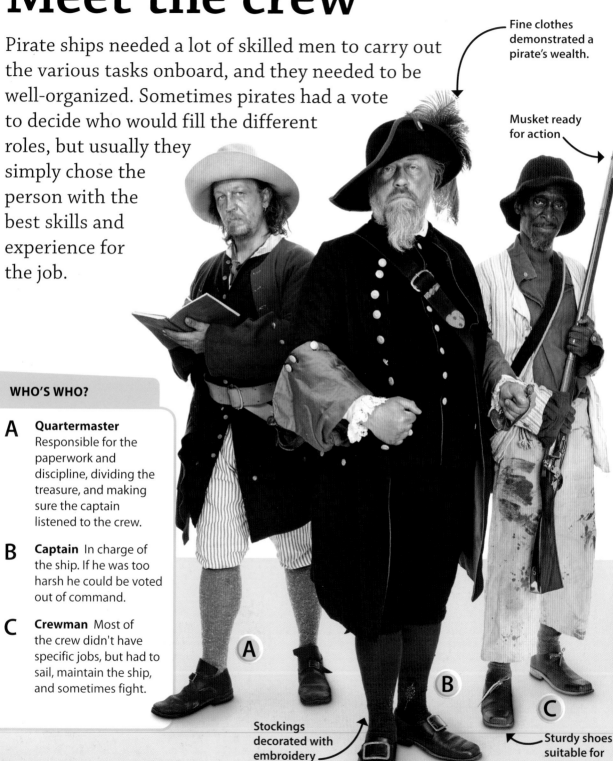

Fine clothes demonstrated a pirate's wealth.

Musket ready for action

WHO'S WHO?

A **Quartermaster** Responsible for the paperwork and discipline, dividing the treasure, and making sure the captain listened to the crew.

B **Captain** In charge of the ship. If he was too harsh he could be voted out of command.

C **Crewman** Most of the crew didn't have specific jobs, but had to sail, maintain the ship, and sometimes fight.

Stockings decorated with embroidery

Sturdy shoes suitable for life at sea

Pirate crews varied from just **a few people** to **several hundred**.

Special woolly hats, called "thrummed caps," kept pirates very warm.

Carpenters wore practical clothes.

WHO'S WHO?

D **Carpenter** In charge of making sure the wooden ship was kept in good condition and repairing any damage.

E **Gunner** Kept the cannon working and trained men to load and fire guns.

F **Forced man** Not everyone wanted to be a pirate. Sometimes men with particular skills, such as musicians, were forced to join the crew!

G **Ship's boy** Some pirate crews included boys. They got a small share of the treasure for doing jobs such as cooking, sewing, and cleaning.

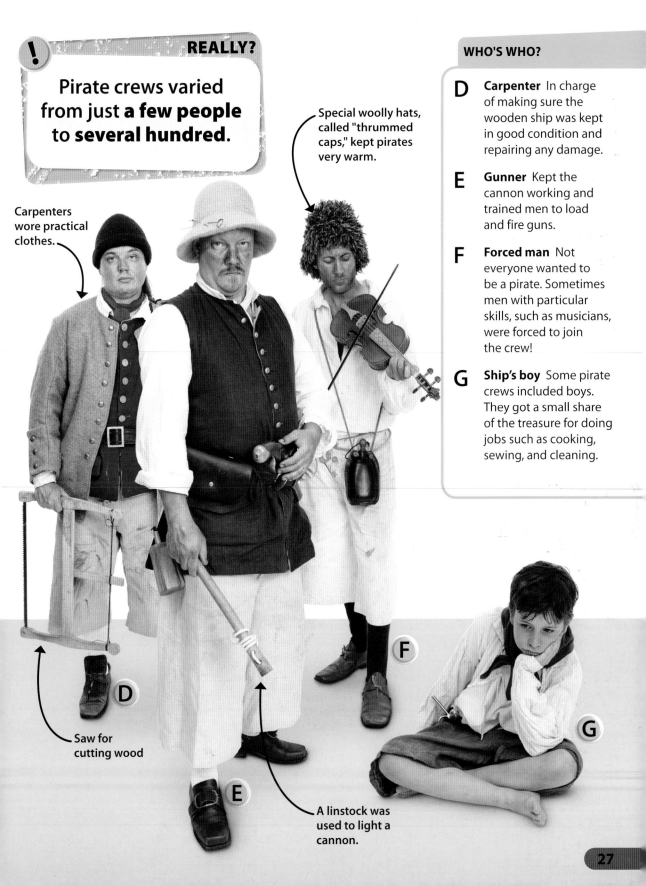

Saw for cutting wood

A linstock was used to light a cannon.

Weapons

Pirates preferred to frighten their victims, rather than fight them. But when they had to fight, they used a wide range of weapons. As their guns could only fire one shot before reloading, pirates often carried several guns, dropping each one after firing it.

Grenade

Grenades were cast-iron balls filled with gunpowder and fitted with a fuse. The flame traveled down the lit fuse to the gunpowder, which exploded, sending pieces of iron flying through the air.

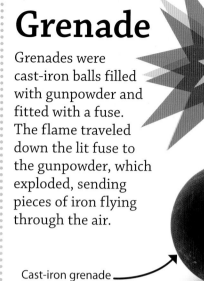

Cast-iron grenade

Pistols were made of wood, but had a metal firing mechanism.

Pistol

Pirates often carried several pistols. Blackbeard famously carried six! Sometimes they were looped around the neck on a ribbon. This meant they would not be lost when they were dropped after firing their single shot.

Ax

Axes were cheap and useful tools around a ship. They also made a very effective and deadly weapon in battle!

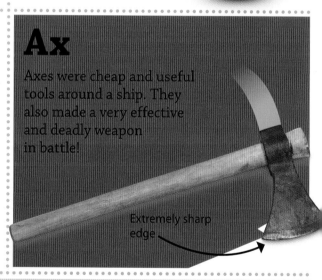

Extremely sharp edge

Cutlass

Once they had fired all of their guns, pirates usually relied on a cutlass, a short, slightly curved sword. Machetes and sugar cane-cutting knives were also used when cutlasses were not available.

A guard was fitted to protect the user's hand.

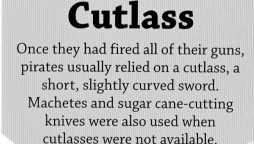

A short blade was easier to use in the confined spaces found onboard ships.

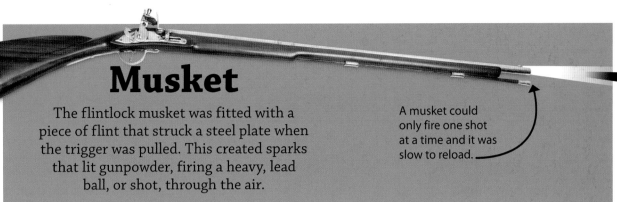

Musket

The flintlock musket was fitted with a piece of flint that struck a steel plate when the trigger was pulled. This created sparks that lit gunpowder, firing a heavy, lead ball, or shot, through the air.

A musket could only fire one shot at a time and it was slow to reload.

This small cannon could be turned to face any direction. The handle, or "tiller," was used to aim the cannon.

Cannons were usually made of iron or bronze.

Cannon

Most pirate ships had several cannons of different sizes. Each one needed between two and five men to load and fire it, which took several minutes.

Gunpowder and shot were loaded through the muzzle end.

Types of shot

Pirates loaded different types of shot into their cannons. Which type of shot depended on which part of an enemy's ship or boat they were hoping to damage, or whether their main target was the crew itself.

Round shot
This heavy iron ball could tear a large hole in a ship's side.

Bar shot
On firing, bar shot spun around, slicing up sails and rigging.

Grape shot
A tightly packed bag of small metal balls, it was lethal when fired.

Rules

A pirate ship was a dangerous place to work, so it was important that pirates had rules. These rules, called "articles," were signed by every member of the crew to show that they all agreed to them. Here are a few of the most popular rules.

He that sees a sail first shall have the best pistol onboard that ship

The prize of the best pistol on a victim's ship encouraged pirates to keep a good lookout. Sometimes the first aboard was also rewarded.

No fighting onboard the ship! All quarrels to be settled on shore with sword and pistol

To avoid violent brawls, crew members had to wait until land before fighting. However, they often sorted out their differences before then.

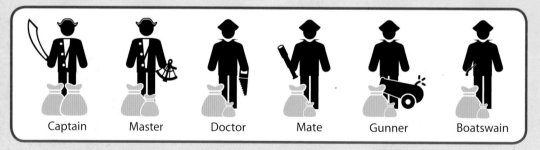

Captain   Master   Doctor   Mate   Gunner   Boatswain

The Captain is to have two full shares; the Master, one share and a half; The Doctor, Mate, Gunner and Boatswain, one share and a quarter

Agreeing how much booty each member of the pirate crew would get, and making sure it was divided fairly, prevented arguments.

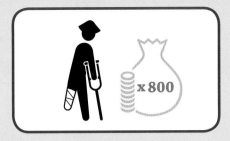

If any man should lose a leg or arm he will receive 800 pieces of eight

An injured pirate would have a hard time making a living ashore, so the crew would make sure they had enough money to survive.

No victim who surrenders is to be harmed

Pirates wanted their victims to surrender so there wouldn't be a fight, but they'd only do that if they thought they would be treated fairly.

If any man shall steal anything in the company, he shall be marooned or shot

Nothing started a fight like stealing from a fellow pirate, so it was strictly banned. Unwise thieves were left alone on an island or killed!

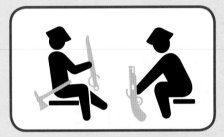

Every man shall keep his weapons clean, and fit for battle, or shall lose his share

Pirates needed to be ready for a scuffle at a moment's notice. Weapons had to be fit for use or they wouldn't get their share of the plunder.

No person to game at cards or dice for money

Unpaid gambling debts could lead to fighting. Pirates avoided this by banning gambling onboard the ship.

Lights and candles to be put out at eight o'clock at night

Running a pirate ship was hard work, so it was important pirates got enough sleep by going to bed on time!

Punishments

To keep order onboard the ship, pirates had to be prepared to punish their own crew. Members of the crew were punished if they broke ship rules, for example if they stole from each other. Some pirates claimed that they had only turned to piracy in the first place because of the cruel punishments on merchant and navy ships. Unfortunately for them, the punishments handed out by pirates were often far worse!

Marooned

Some pirates were punished by being left on a deserted island or empty coast, with only some water and a gun. If they were lucky they could survive long enough to be rescued, but they often died of thirst or hunger.

Marooned pirates were given a gun with one shot. Some chose to shoot themselves, a quicker death than starving!

! WOW!

There are **no records** of pirates actually being made to **walk the plank.**

Alexander Selkirk

Selkirk voluntarily marooned himself in 1704 on one of the Juan Fernández Islands, in the Pacific Ocean, after an argument with his captain. He was eventually rescued after more than four years, and his story inspired novelist Daniel Defoe to write the book *Robinson Crusoe*.

Selkirk trying to attract attention

Hanging

The worst crimes were punished by death. Sometimes this meant shooting, but more often it meant hanging, which was a slower death. Some pirates also hanged their victims.

Hanging was also known as "dancing the hempen jig."

Fines

Lesser crimes could be punished by taking money from a pirate's share of the loot. Since pirates were really in it for the money, nobody wanted to lose out.

Fines hit pirates where it hurt—in the purse!

Cat-o'-nine-tails

In the navy and onboard merchant ships, flogging, or whipping, was usually limited to twelve lashes. For pirates, however, the standard number was 39!

The cat-o'-nine-tails whip left nasty cuts on a man's back.

33

Dinnertime

When a ship first left port, there might be plenty of fresh meat, eggs, and vegetables onboard, but these would soon go moldy! Unless there was a chance to dock and buy fresh supplies, or a ship carrying fresh goods was raided, a pirate crew often had to rely on dried or salted food, which lasted longer.

! WOW!

Pirates would sometimes **raid fishing boats, just to get a fresh supply of fish!**

Dried food
Pasta, beans, peas, and lentils were all foods that could survive a long time at sea.

Beans

Salted pork
Covering meat in salt stopped bacteria and mold growing on it, so it did not spoil.

Peas

Lentils

Preserved food

A pirate crew might spend months at sea, so they needed food that would keep well for a long time. There were no fridges in the Golden Age of Piracy. Food was usually preserved by either drying it or covering it in salt.

Rice
Dried grains of rice not only lasted well, but were also easy to store in large quantities.

Barrels
Everything from meat to rum was stored in tightly sealed wooden casks. They were broken open and resealed as needed.

Limes
Because of its health benefits, lime juice was sometimes more expensive than wine or rum.

Citrus fruit
Pirates didn't know that a lack of vitamin C, found in citrus fruit, caused the deadly disease scurvy—but they knew citrus fruit kept them healthy!

Hunting turtles
Turtles were easy to catch and keep alive onboard, ready to provide fresh meat as required. The pirates would turn them over onto their backs to prevent them from escaping back into the sea.

Turning over a turtle

Salmagundi
Any fresh food available was often served as a salad called salmagundi, which might include meat, fish, eggs, vegetables, fruit, and nuts.

Fresh food
After months of dried and salted food, a dish including fresh vegetables was a rare treat.

Female pirates

Very few pirate crews included women and they were banned from some ships completely, but a few female pirates did exist. The most famous were Anne Bonny and Mary Read, who both sailed with the pirate captain "Calico Jack" Rackham. They are best known for dressing up as men when they went into battle.

"Stays" were stiffened items of clothing that gave women a fashionable shape.

Dressed as a female

Contrary to popular belief, Bonny and Read were not disguised as men all of the time. When they weren't fighting they wore regular women's clothes on deck.

The "mantua" was a warm top garment a bit like a coat.

Women wore several layers of skirts, called "petticoats."

! REALLY?

Bonny and Read **escaped execution** because they were both **pregnant**.

Leather shoes and woolen stockings completed the outfit.

Pictures from the time show Bonny and Read wearing felt "round hats."

Dressed as a male

Bonny and Read wore men's clothing in battle. This was probably because it was easier to fight in men's clothes, but also because they thought people would be less frightened of them if they wore ladies' clothes.

Axes were a useful tool onboard a ship.

It was easier to fight in pants than a skirt!

A picture of Bonny and Read from 1724

Bonny and Read

Bonny and Read were only pirates for a few weeks before they were captured, but they were famous for their courage and brutality toward their victims. Mary Read died in prison in Jamaica, while Anne Bonny's fate remains a mystery to this day.

Henry Every

On a single trip, Captain Every and his men captured a fortune in coins and jewels. They had stolen from a ship owned by the king of India himself, and a worldwide hunt for the pirate was launched. Every managed to escape and was never found, making him one of the most successful pirates in history.

Gang-i-Sawai
The magnificent *Gang-i-Sawai* was the biggest ship in the Indian fleet and carried the richest passengers.

Who was Henry Every?
Every began his career as an officer in the British Royal Navy. He became a privateer, and then a pirate captain.

! WOW!

The hunt for Every stretched over **four continents!**

What did he do?
Every knew about a yearly Indian fleet that was full of treasure. The fleet carried rich people to visit Mecca, a religious destination for pilgrims. Every sailed to the Red Sea, where he knew the fleet would pass.

Fight!
When the fleet arrived, there was a long chase and a few hours of fighting. Every's men captured the fleet's largest ship, the *Gang-i-Sawai*.

Mystery
Every returned to England and disappeared. He was never found and his fate remains a mystery to this day!

Crew captured
The British joined a huge chase for Every. Several of his crew were captured, and eight were executed.

Kennack Sands

Some people believed Every hid his treasure at Kennack Sands in Cornwall.

British East India Company
The Mughal ordered a search for Every. He threatened to kick the British East India Company, which traded Indian goods, out of India.

Treasure you say?
Onboard were fabulous treasures including gold, silver, and jewels. Every's men all became rich.

The Mughal was angry
The ship was owned by the Grand Mughal (king) of India. He was outraged that his ship had been attacked by pirates.

Pirate hunters

Pirates were declared "the enemies of all mankind" in the 17th century. The world's navies and pirate hunters sailed the oceans trying to capture them, sometimes very successfully. Pirates who were caught could not expect much mercy. In England they were thrown into Marshalsea Prison. There they awaited trial and, if found guilty, execution. A merry life, but often a short one!

The Royal Navy

The Royal Navy of Great Britain sent ships to hunt pirates around the world. In the 18th century, they kept a number of warships in the Caribbean just for that purpose.

Captain Kidd

Kidd sailed from England to hunt pirates in the Indian Ocean. After discovering that piracy was more profitable, he became one of the most fearsome pirates of the age!

Benjamin Hornigold betrayed his fellow pirates to **become a pirate hunter!**

Pirate punishments

Some lucky pirates were pardoned after being captured, which meant they were let off for their crimes. Most were executed, but a few escaped this fate by agreeing to work as slaves in African gold mines.

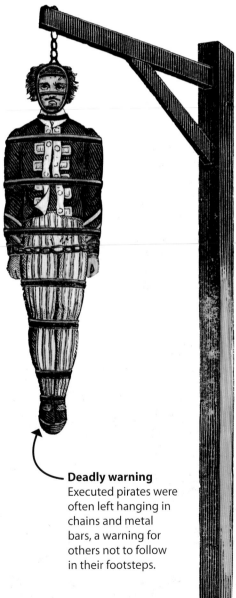

Woodes Rogers

Rogers volunteered as a privateer, working on behalf of the British government to evict pirates from their base in the Bahamas. He was very successful, becoming the archenemy of the pirates.

Deadly warning
Executed pirates were often left hanging in chains and metal bars, a warning for others not to follow in their footsteps.

Bartholomew Roberts

Bartholomew Roberts was one of the most successful pirates of the Golden Age. In a career of less than three years he captured more than 400 ships, and seemed invincible. Despite his fearsome reputation he had a taste for fancy clothes!

! WOW!

Roberts did not like **rum**—he preferred to drink **tea**!

Finery
When going into battle Roberts liked to dress in patterned silk clothes, and wore a diamond cross around his neck.

Kidnapped!
Roberts began his career when he was captured by the pirate Howell Davis and forced to join his crew.

Voted captain
As an experienced navigator Roberts was highly valued by the crew. When Davis was killed in battle the crew voted for Roberts to be their new captain.

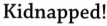

Astrolabe for navigating

When Bart attacks

Roberts' flagship, the *Royal Rover*, had more than 30 cannons. Together with the rest of the ships under his command it made a terrifying sight.

Tactics

As well as having a powerful fleet, Roberts was a clever man. He always put his ships in the best position in a fight to make sure he won.

Pirate legend

Roberts was famous during his lifetime, and his great successes made him the most feared pirate in the world. Fame came at a price, however, and the British Royal Navy sent two warships to hunt him down.

The last battle

The British ship HMS *Swallow* found Roberts with his ships at anchor on the African coast. Roberts was killed in the following battle and his body was thrown overboard.

Work and play

Between capturing other ships, pirates had a lot of spare time. Much of it was taken up with important tasks and routines, such as repairing and cleaning their ship. However they also had a lot of time to relax, so they came up with different ways to avoid getting bored.

Playing cards

Pirates were not usually allowed to gamble for money, but they still enjoyed card and dice games as a way to pass the time.

MUSIC

Some pirates played music, while others practiced with their weapons, and they all loved to sing in the evenings. Violins and drums were popular instruments, and they would sometimes be played during battle.

Cleaning

This isn't much fun...

Keeping the ship clean was important to prevent disease. Quite often it was the boys, slaves, or forced men who had to do this work.

Gun care

Flintlock guns, which used a piece of flint to create a spark, were complicated and required constant maintenance. Pirates who didn't keep their guns clean could be punished by the crew.

A pirate cleaning his flintlock pistol with a fine brush.

Pirates were skilled at patching and sewing sails.

A bullet mold and bullets

Ammunition

All the guns required ammunition. Lead bullets could easily be made onboard by melting lead over a fire and then pouring it into a special mold.

Sailmaking

Without sails a ship couldn't get very far, so they had to be kept in good condition at all times. One pirate crew ran out of canvas, which was the usual material for making sails, so used silk instead!

Drinking

More than anything else pirates loved to get drunk. Their favorite drink was brandy, but rum, wine, or a mixture called "punch," were also popular.

Caulking

To stop a ship from leaking, pirates had to fill the seams between the planks with old rope fibers and tar. This process is called "caulking." To reach the seams near the bottom of the ship pirates had to pull it over onto one side!

Mischief

Pirates played a lot of silly games. Swearing competitions were common, and when one crew captured some monks they raced them around the ship, riding on their shoulders!

Sails

Pirate junk
The most common sailing
vessel in Asian waters was
called a "junk." The sails were
stiffened with bamboo strips,
which made them easier to
roll up. These boats are still
in operation today.

Crew

Cargo

Helm

思永川

Pirates of the Far East

The trade in silks and spices in the waters around Asia provided
an ideal hunting ground for pirates from China, Japan, Borneo,
and Indonesia. Long coastlines and deep jungles were perfect
places for the pirates to hide, ready to launch attacks on
merchant ships in their sailing junks and long war-canoes.

Pirate queen

The Chinese pirate Ching Shih (1775–1844) took charge of her husband's fleet following his death. She was a huge success, and at one point commanded more than 40,000 men!

Ching Shih terrorized the China Sea.

Gunpowder was invented by **Chinese monks** in the ninth century.

Pirate hunter

James Brooke was an English adventurer who fought pirates in Borneo. To thank him, the Sultan made him Rajah (king) of the Sarawak region.

James Brooke (1803–1868)

Chinese chief

Wang Zhi was a Chinese pirate chief based in Japan who raided his own countrymen. In 1559, he was caught by the Chinese government and executed.

Wang Zhi is famous for introducing the first Europeans to Japan in the 16th century.

Dress like a pirate

Pirates dressed in clothes that were popular in society at the time. Because life at sea was tough, their clothes had to be practical and hard-wearing. Sailors, including pirates, had their own styles when it came to what to wear.

A felt hat with a brim protected pirates from the sun's glare.

Fashionable coat made of coarse wool

Sword held in a thick, strong leather belt

Long woolen waistcoat. It is believed that sailors invented pockets!

Knee-length breeches made of strong fabric called "ticking"

Leather shoes with brass buckles

REALLY?

Pirates usually **stole their clothes** from the sailors they **captured**.

Officers

Pirate leaders, called officers, wore practical clothes, as did their crew. However, because their work was less physical than regular crewmen's, they could wear more stylish and fashionable garments.

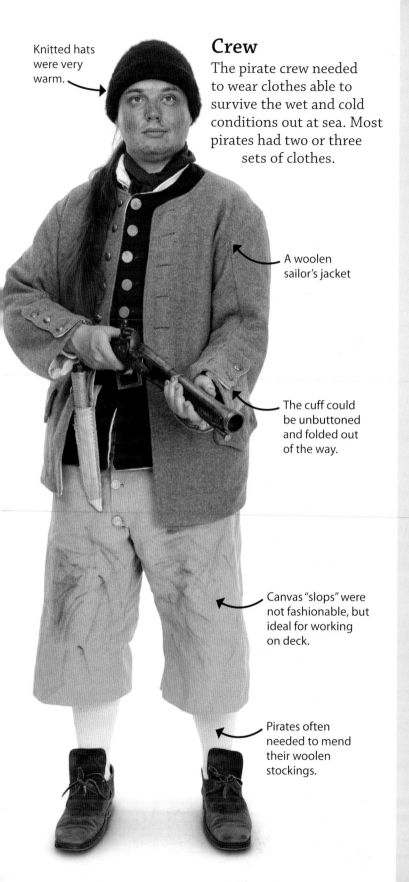

Knitted hats were very warm.

Crew

The pirate crew needed to wear clothes able to survive the wet and cold conditions out at sea. Most pirates had two or three sets of clothes.

A woolen sailor's jacket

The cuff could be unbuttoned and folded out of the way.

Canvas "slops" were not fashionable, but ideal for working on deck.

Pirates often needed to mend their woolen stockings.

Step by step

There were many layers to a pirate's outfit. They often slept in their undergarments, so dressing in the morning was a simple process.

Undergarments
Undergarments consisted of a linen shirt, a pair of linen "drawers" (underwear), and woolen stockings.

Waistcoat and slops
The next thing to go on were the canvas slops, followed by a waistcoat with a belt over the top.

Stock and shoes
Shoes went on next, then a linen "stock." This was a type of neck cloth that provided warmth and protection from the sun.

Jacket and hat
Finally the pirate put on his jacket and hat. Important possessions were probably kept in the jacket pockets.

Interview with **Blackbeard**

Pirate tyrant

FACT FILE

» **Name:** Edward Teach

» **Dates:** c.1690–1718

» **Location:** The Caribbean and the American coast

Edward Teach, more commonly known as Blackbeard, was one of the most famous pirates in history. For two years he terrorized the Caribbean and American coast, at one point holding a whole town for ransom. After he was killed, his head was publically displayed to prove he was dead.

Q: Blackbeard, why do you think you became so famous?

A: I knew that being a pirate would be easier if everyone was already frightened of me, so I made a lot of effort to get myself known.

Q: Did your huge beard help?

A: Not many people had beards in my day, so it was a way of becoming recognized and remembered. The beard was my trademark.

Q: How did you become so powerful and feared in America?

A: My flagship, *Queen Anne's Revenge*, was the biggest pirate ship in the region, and I had other ships with me, too.

Q: How did you keep command over your enormous crew?

A: I gave them success! And if that didn't work I would occasionally shoot one, just to remind them who was in charge.

Q: Where were you born?

A: It's a mystery. I had family in Jamaica, and used to work in Philadelphia in America, but I was probably born in the port of Bristol, England.

Q: Do you ever feel bad about robbing and killing people?

A: Not really. I didn't often kill people, but would hurt them to get what I want.

Q: Did you ever sell slaves?

A: Yes, slaves were worth a lot of money! I sold 50 of them when I tried to retire in North Carolina on the American coast.

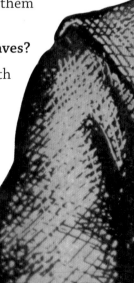

Let's jump on board, and cut them to pieces!

Lit fuses in Blackbeard's hair made an intimidating sight.

Q: What was your greatest achievement?

A: I held Charleston, South Carolina, to ransom for several days because my crew needed a medicine chest. That really made my name as a pirate.

Q: What's your secret to success?

A: Due to my reputation, nobody wanted to fight the notorious Blackbeard! I would put burning matches in my hair when I boarded a ship, and that used to terrify people. People practically gave me their stuff after that.

Q: Do you have any regrets?

A: If I'd quit while I was ahead I might not have been killed.

Blackbeard was finally killed in a fierce battle with British Naval forces commanded by Robert Maynard.

Meet the expert

David Moore is a maritime archaeologist and historian who specializes in shipwrecks. In 1996 he helped locate the wreck of the *Queen Anne's Revenge*—Blackbeard's legendary flagship. He continues to study it to this day.

Q: We know it's something to do with pirate ships, but what is your actual job?

A: My position with the North Carolina Maritime Museum is the Curator of Nautical Archaeology. Most of my duties entail working on the Queen Anne's Revenge Shipwreck Project, which includes diving on the site and mapping the wreck remains.

Q: How did you first get interested in pirates?

A: Like many people, I've always had a general interest in the exploits of pirates. As an undergraduate in college I read a

David Moore exploring a shipwreck

biography on Blackbeard and that solidified my personal interest in piracy.

Q: What made you want to become an underwater archaeologist?

A: After graduating in 1980 with a degree in marine science, I participated in an underwater archaeology field school that same summer. During the course of our investigations we located and examined two shipwrecks. I was immediately fascinated by the potential of studying shipwrecks as a profession.

Q: When you're on the seabed, what an you actually see?

A: The *Queen Anne's Revenge* shipwreck site is subjected to tidal flow [currents in the water caused by the tides], which means that visibility on the site is normally restricted to about 3–4 ft (1–1.2 m).

Q: When you find something big, say, a cannon, how do you get it out of the water?

A: Before recovery, a cannon is totally excavated to make sure that additional objects are not attached that might make moving it more problematic. Then heavy-duty straps are wrapped around the barrel and attached to a lifting bag, to float the gun off the site. The gun is then hooked up to a crane on the boat, lifted clear of the water, and placed on large wooden blocks set on the deck.

Q: What is the best thing that's happened to you at work?

A: The locating and eventually identifying of Blackbeard's flagship *Queen Anne's Revenge*, particularly after proposing to look for the wreck so many years ago and having no one take it seriously!

Q: What is the worst thing that's happened to you at work?

A: Although I've never been seriously injured while at work, I did suffer a burst eardrum about eight years ago. Making four or five dives a day down about 25 ft (8 m) to the site can put your inner ear through a workout.

Lifting a cannon onto the deck

Q: What amazing things have you found from the *Queen Anne's Revenge*?

A: One cool item was gold dust recovered from the site. We know that the slave ship *Concorde* had in excess of 20 lbs (9 kg) of gold dust onboard when captured by Blackbeard. So recovering gold dust from the site was no real surprise.

Q: Do you have a favorite pirate?

A: Because he left at least three shipwrecks here in North Carolina waters where I work, and the fact that we have been working on his flagship, I would have to say Blackbeard.

Q: . If we wanted to become an underwater archaeologist, what would we need to do?

A: If you're serious about becoming an underwater archaeologist, you should obtain a certification in SCUBA diving. You should also get an undergraduate degree in marine sciences, history, or archaeology, and probably a Master's degree in a similar discipline.

Raising the anchor

Life on land

Pirates could not spend all of their time at sea. They needed to be able to repair their vessels, stock up on supplies, and have somewhere to spend their treasure. There were a choice of pirate ports they could head to—and special reasons why they would pick each one.

Good

- Nassau gave the pirates easy access to rich Atlantic trade routes.
- A strong fort protected ships at anchor in the harbor.

Nassau

The Bahamas were a British colony, but in 1716 the authorities lost control of the islands to pirates. The pirates made their headquarters in the capital Nassau, until they were evicted by Woodes Rogers in 1718.

The Bahamas are located in the Caribbean Sea.

Bad

- British authorities could not allow the pirates to remain in control.
- Many inhabitants opposed the pirates' presence in the islands.

- Pirates could stay in the region for years at a time.
- No European government could evict the pirates from the island.

Good

- The trading post charged high prices for the available goods.
- Angry natives eventually drove the pirates from the island.

Bad

Isle St. Marie

A trading post was set up on an island off the coast of Madagascar. Here pirates could trade their loot for useful supplies, such as food, gunpowder, books, and clothing.

Madagascar is an island off Africa.

Good

- A friendly government welcomed buccaneers of all nations.
- A fort in the harbor protected the buccaneers' vessels.

Bad

- Buccaneers fighting among themselves made Tortuga a very dangerous place.
- The French government eventually kicked the buccaneers off the island.

Tortuga

Seventeenth-century buccaneers helped to secure the Caribbean island Tortuga for the French, and were allowed to use it as a base.

Tortuga is located in the Caribbean Sea.

Are there still pirates?

You might think you're safe from a pirate attack in the modern world, but piracy was common throughout the 20th century and still takes place today. As long as there are ships on the world's oceans and lakes, there will be pirates trying to capture them.

"Roaring" Dan Seavey

Dan Seavey was an early 20th-century pirate who sailed on the Great Lakes of North America. He raided ships in the harbor at night, kidnapped women, and hijacked boats sailing on the lakes.

Felix von Luckner

German Felix von Luckner famously captured 14 British merchant ships during the First World War. He was caught near New Zealand in 1917, escaped the same year, and then was captured again!

Malacca Straits

More than one-third of all trade ships in the world pass through a narrow stretch of water called the Malacca Straits, in Southeast Asia. This attracts pirates to the area, and in 2015 more than 125 ships were attacked in this area alone.

FACT FILE

» **Location:** South East Asian waters

» **Active:** Throughout time

Somali pirates

Using fast boats, machine guns, and rocket launchers, pirates from Somalia in East Africa are well-known for hijacking cargo ships and kidnapping passengers.

FACT FILE

» **Location:** Somalian coast, East Africa

» **Active:** 2005–present

Piracy in numbers

What we know about pirates often comes from the records of survivors. Impress your friends with these amazing facts!

$318,000,000

Estimated cost in today's money of the richest prize captured by pirates, the *Nuestra Señora de la Cabo*. It was taken by Richard Taylor and Olivier la Buse in 1721.

52

Pirates hung at Cabo Corso, Africa, in 1722, the most executed at one time during the Golden Age.

144

Number of men drowned when the pirate ship *Whydah* sank in 1717.

50

Number of cannons on the pirate ship *Speaker*.

20,000

Number of pirates under the command of Ching Shih.

5,000

Pirates estimated to have been active during the **Golden Age**.

Days spent by the crew of the Golden Hind sailing around the world.

1,020

400

Number of ships captured by **Bartholomew Roberts**

108

Number of villagers kidnapped in the largest attack by Barbary pirates on a settlement in Ireland or Britain.

22

Number of merchant ships abandoned by their crews when Bartholomew Roberts approached Trepassy Harbor, Canada, in 1720.

400

Number of pirates in Blackbeard's crew.

Glossary

These words will be useful to know when finding out all about pirates and their adventures on the seven seas.

articles Set of rules followed by pirates onboard a ship

bow Front of a ship

broadside Cannons placed along one side of a ship

buccaneers Pig-hunters and soldiers on land who became pirates in the Caribbean Sea

captain Person in charge of a ship

cargo Goods carried onboard a ship

colony Area of land or island belonging to a different country

corsair Name given to Mediterranean pirates

crew Group of people who work on a ship

deck Floor of a ship

fleet Several ships sailing together

flintlock Type of gun that lets off sparks when fired

flogging Whipping, used as a punishment

frigate Type of fast, three-masted ship

galleon Large sailing ship with a high deck at each end

galley Ship that is rowed using oars

gambling Playing games to win (or lose) money

governor Government official in charge of an island or colony

hanging Deadly punishment in which a person is hung from a rope around their neck

hold Area of a ship used for storage

Jolly Roger A pirate ship's flag

junk Type of Asian sailing ship

loot Money or goods stolen by pirates, sometimes called plunder

merchant Someone who swaps or sells goods

A junk

Loot

merchant ship Ship that carries goods from one place to another

musket Large gun that could shoot objects that are faraway

muzzle Front end of a gun or cannon

navy Collection of warships owned by a government

notorious Famous or well-known

officer Person with extra responsibility and authority on a ship

pardon When a criminal is forgiven by a government and allowed to go free

piracy Stealing at sea

pirate Person who steals at sea

pistol Small gun that can be fired at nearby objects

plunder Stolen cargo, such as goods or money

port Waterside town or city where ships sail from

privateer Someone given permission to commit piracy by a government

provisions Food, drink, and other things needed by a ship's crew while at sea

rigging Ropes on a ship that hold up masts and control sails

rum Alcoholic drink made from sugar cane

sails Large pieces of fabric that catch the wind to help move a ship forward

scurvy Deadly illness caused by a lack of vitamin C

silk Expensive fabric from Asia

slave Person forced to work for someone else

slaver Type of ship used to transport slaves. It was usually fast-moving and well-armed

sloop Small, fast, single-masted vessel

stern Back of a ship

trade route Route sailed by merchant ships carrying goods from one country to another

vessel Boat or ship

windward In the direction from which the wind is blowing

Pirate ships carried barrels of wine as a provision.

Index

Acknowledgments

DORLING KINDERSLEY would like to thank: Suneha Dutta for editorial assistance, Fiona Macdonald, Nehal Varma, Shubham Rohatgi, Sachin Singh, and Vijay Kandwal for design assistance, Polly Goodman for proofreading, and Helen Peters for the index. The publishers would also like to thank David Moore for the "Meet the expert" interview, Lol Johnson for photography, Juliana Sergot for make-up, Ed Fox, Zachary Wright, Kathleen Teece, Sam Priddy, Tim Eagling, Jonathan Terris, Anthony Limerick, and Edward Leighton for modelling, and Andrew Kerr and Maltings Partnership for their illustrations.

The publisher would like to thank the following for their kind permission to reproduce their photographs:

(Key: a-above; b-below/bottom; c-centre; f-far; l-left; r-right; t-top)

4 Alamy Stock Photo: North Wind Picture Archives (cb). **5 Alamy Stock Photo:** Berthier Emmanuel / hemis.fr (tl). **Bridgeman Images:** Private Collection / © Look and Learn / Illustrated Papers Collection (bl). **7 Alamy Stock Photo:** Photos 12 (clb); Marek Uliasz (cla); Matt Smith (br). **10 Bridgeman Images:** Zev Radovan (tl). **11 Alamy Stock Photo:** Granger, NYC. / Granger Historical Picture Archve (c). **Bridgeman Images:** Jaquerio, Giacomo (fl.1403-53) / Castello della Manta, Saluzzo, Italy (cr); Musee du Bardo, Tunis, Tunisia (bc). **12-13 Alamy Stock Photo:** Danny Smythe. **14 Alamy Stock Photo:** Falkensteinfoto (cr). **Getty Images:** Joel W. Rogers / Corbis Documentary (cb). **14-15 Alamy Stock Photo:** Falkensteinfoto. **15 Alamy Stock Photo:** North Wind Picture Archives (crb). **Dorling Kindersley:** Canterbury City Council, Museums and Galleries (br). **Getty Images:** Universal Images Group (c). **16-17 Bridgeman Images:** Private Collection. **18 Alamy Stock Photo:** Jason Smalley Photography (tr). **Aland Maritime Museum:** (b). **20 Confederate Memorial Hall, New Orleans, LA:** (fclb). **Dorling Kindersley:** James Young (cr/nutmeg). **Getty Images:** Carlos Gawronski / E+ (c). **20-21 Alamy Stock Photo:** Jon Helgason. **21 Getty Images:** Culture Club / Hulton Archive (cra); Interim Archives / Archive Photos (crb); Visage / Stockbyte (cl/pot). **22 Alamy Stock Photo:** Granger, NYC. / Granger Historical Picture Archve (cr). **Fotolia:** picsfive (fcl, c). **23 Alamy Stock Photo:** nsf (bl). **Fotolia:** picsfive (tl). **24-25 Dorling Kindersley:** Andrew Kerr. **32-33 Bridgeman Images:** Delaware Art Museum, Wilmington, USA / Museum Purchase. **32 Alamy Stock Photo:** Granger, NYC. / Granger Historical Picture Archve (crb). **33 Alamy Stock Photo:** Big Pants Productions (tr). **35 Getty Images:** Science & Society Picture Library / SSPL (tr). **37 Alamy Stock Photo:** Lebrecht Music and Arts Photo Library (crb). **38-39 Getty Images:** Culture Club / Hulton Archive. **39 Alamy Stock Photo:** Deeplyvibed (c). **40 Alamy Stock Photo:** Granger, NYC. / Granger Historical Picture Archve (r). **Bridgeman Images:** Private Collection (l).

41 Alamy Stock Photo: North Wind Picture Archives (r). **Photo Scala, Florence:** Photo Art Media / Heritage Images (l). **42 Alamy Stock Photo:** Lebrecht Music and Arts Photo Library (r). **43 Alamy Stock Photo:** Lebrecht Music and Arts Photo Library (t). **45 Alamy Stock Photo:** Granger, NYC. / Granger Historical Picture Archve (cr); Lanmas (cl). **Getty Images:** Ullstein Bild (br). **46 Alamy Stock Photo:** Sybil Sassoon / robertharding (br). **47 Alamy Stock Photo:** Ian Dagnall (bl); Lebrecht Music and Arts Photo Library (tl); Granger, NYC. / Granger Historical Picture Archve (cr). **Dorling Kindersley:** The Science Museum, London (cra). **50-51 Bridgeman Images:** Private Collection / Peter Newark Historical Pictures. **51 Bridgeman Images:** Private Collection (crb). **52 David Moore:** (tr, bl). **52-53 Fotolia:** Malbert. **53 Alamy Stock Photo:** US Coast Guard Photo (tr). **Getty Images:** Raleigh News & Observer / Tribune News Service (bl). **54 Getty Images:** Print Collector / Hulton Archive (c). **55 Getty Images:** Print Collector / Hulton Archive (crb). **Mary Evans Picture Library:** (t). **56 Alamy Stock Photo:** akg-images (br); Granger, NYC. / Granger Historical Picture Archve (crb). **Getty Images:** Chicago History Museum / Archive Photos (cl). **57 Getty Images:** Adek Berry / AFP (cr); Veronique de Viguerie / Reportage Archive (bl). **58 Alamy Stock Photo:** North Wind Picture Archives (tr). **59 Alamy Stock Photo:** Lebrecht Music and Arts Photo Library (cla, bl). **Bridgeman Images:** Private Collection / Peter Newark Historical Pictures (br). **60 Alamy Stock Photo:** Sybil Sassoon / robertharding (bc). **Photo Scala, Florence:** Photo Art Media / Heritage Images (tl).

Cover images: Front: Dorling Kindersley: National Maritime Museum, London cr; *Front Flap:* **Alamy Stock Photo:** Big Pants Productions cla; *Back Flap:* **Dorling Kindersley:** Natural History Museum, London cra, Natural History Museum, London crb; **NASA:** clb; *Front Endpapers:* **Alamy Stock Photo:** GL Archive 0 (1536), Granger, NYC. / Granger Historical Picture Archve 0 (66 BCE), Interfoto / Personalities 0 (1400), Nawrocki / ClassicStock 0 (1698), Anthony Pleva 0 (1715), Prisma Archivo 0 (410 CE), World History Archive 0 (1695); **Getty Images:** De Agostini Picture Library / De Agostini 0 (1577); **Rex by Shutterstock:** De Agostini / G. Lovera 0 (1175 BCE); *Back Endpapers:* **Alamy Stock Photo:**

Ian Dagnall 0 (1841), GL Archive 0 (1883), Lebrecht Music and Arts Photo Library 0 (1720), 0 (1724), Photo Researchers, Inc 0 (1807), Jim West 0 (1814), World History Archive 0 (1722); **Getty Images:** Hulton Archive 0 (1904); **Photoshot:** Laura Moore / Lightroom / US Navy 0 (2009).

Endpapers: *Front:* **Alamy Stock Photo:** GL Archive (1536); Granger, NYC. / Granger Historical Picture Archve (66 BCE); Interfoto / Personalities (1400); Nawrocki / ClassicStock (1698); Anthony Pleva (1715); Prisma Archivo (410 CE); World History Archive (1695). **Getty Images:** De Agostini Picture Library / De Agostini (1577). **Rex by Shutterstock:** De Agostini / G. Lovera (1175 BCE). *Back:* **Alamy Stock Photo:** Ian Dagnall (1841); GL Archive (1883); Lebrecht Music and Arts Photo Library (1720), (1724); Photo Researchers, Inc (1807); Jim West (1814); World History Archive (1722). **Getty Images:** Hulton Archive (1904). **Photoshot:** Laura Moore / Lightroom / US Navy (2009).

All other images © Dorling Kindersley
For further information see:
www.dkimages.com

About the author

E.T. Fox, M.A., Ph.D, is a historian and author specialising in the history of pirates and maritime history. He was formerly the curator of the Golden Hind Museum in Brixham, UK. Currently he lives on Dartmoor with two wonderful children and two dogs, where he drinks a lot of tea.

My Findout facts:

Timeline of Pirates

Big loot
Richard Taylor leads the capture of the *Nuestra Señora de la Cabo*, the most valuable prize ever taken by a pirate.

End of Golden Age of Piracy
Edward Low and Francis Spriggs are marooned by their men, marking the end of the Golden Age of Piracy.

Roberts killed
Bartholomew Roberts is killed in battle with HMS *Swallow*. Fifty two of the survivors are later executed.

 Continued from front of book

1720	1721	1722	1724	1726	1729	1807

Bonny and Read
Anne Bonny and Mary Read join the crew of John Rackham. Two months later they are captured and put on trial in Jamaica.

Mary Read kills a sailor who had insulted her.

A GENERAL
HISTORY
OF THE
Robberies and Murders
Of the most notorious
PYRATES,
AND ALSO
Their Policies, Discipline and Government,
From their first Rise and Settlement in the Island of Providence, in 1717, to the present Year 1724.

By Captain CHARLES JOHNSON.

Woman executed for piracy
Maria Crichet, along with five men, is executed in Virginia. She is the only woman executed for piracy in English law.

Red Flag pirates
Ching Shih becomes leader of the Red Flag pirates in China.

Famous book
Publication of Captain Charles Johnson's book, *A General History of the Robberies and Murders of the Most Notorious Pyrates*.